Pip!

Written by Helen Betts

Illustrated by Nanette Regan

Pip can not tag Kit.

Pip can not tag Meg.

Pip can not tag Dot.

Pip can not tag Sam.

Pip can tag Dad!

Talk about the story

Ask your child these questions:

1 Who did Pip try to tag first?

2 Who did Pip follow across the stepping stones?

3 How many mice were playing tag in the woods?

4 Why was Pip able to tag Dad?

5 Do you like playing tag?

6 Have you seen a mouse like Pip in real life?

Can your child retell the story in their own words?